Bugs in My Backyard

I S

Ladybugs

By Julia Jaske

I see a ladybug.

I see a spotted ladybug.

 I see a red ladybug.

I see an orange ladybug.

I see a ladybug flying.

I see a ladybug exploring.

 I see a ladybug eating.

I see a ladybug smelling.

 I see a ladybug drinking.

I see a ladybug climbing.

I see a ladybug relaxing.

I see a ladybug saying hello!

Word List

ladybug

spotted

red

orange

flying

exploring

eating

smelling

drinking

climbing

relaxing

saying

hello

60 Words

I see a ladybug.

I see a spotted ladybug.

I see a red ladybug.

I see an orange ladybug.

I see a ladybug flying.

I see a ladybug exploring.

I see a ladybug eating.

I see a ladybug smelling.

I see a ladybug drinking.

I see a ladybug climbing.

I see a ladybug relaxing.

I see a ladybug saying hello!

Published in the United States of America by Cherry Lake Publishing Group
Ann Arbor, Michigan
www.cherrylakepublishing.com

Book Designer: Melinda Millward

Photo Credits: ©Visual Intermezzo/Shutterstock.com, front cover, 1, 4; ©Alex Staroseltsev/
Shutterstock.com, back cover, 14; © Be Good/Shutterstock.com, 2; ©Pasqua Giacomo/
Shutterstock.com, 3; ©fragariavesca/Shutterstock.com, 5; ©InsectWorld/Shutterstock.com, 6;
©Anatoliy Berislavskiy/Shutterstock.com, 7; ©Jolanda Aalbers/Shutterstock.com, 8; ©Scorpp/
Shutterstock.com, 9; ©yanikap/Shutterstock.com, 10; ©Yevhenii Chulovskyi/Shutterstock.com,
11; ©PHOTO FUN/Shutterstock.com, 12; ©SabOlga/Shutterstock.com, 13

Cherry Blossom Press is an imprint of Cherry Lake Publishing Group.

Library of Congress Cataloging-in-Publication Data

Names: Jaske, Julia, author.
Title: I see ladybugs / by Julia Jaske.
Description: Ann Arbor, Michigan : Cherry Lake Publishing, 2022. | Series: Bugs in my backyard |
    Audience: Grades K-1
Identifiers: LCCN 2021036409 (print) | LCCN 2021036410 (ebook) | ISBN 9781534198845
    (paperback) | ISBN 9781668905746 (ebook) | ISBN 9781668901427 (pdf)
Subjects: LCSH: Ladybugs—Juvenile literature.
Classification: LCC QL596.C65 J335 2022 (print) | LCC QL596.C65 (ebook) | DDC 595.76/9–dc23
LC record available at https://lccn.loc.gov/2021036409
LC ebook record available at https://lccn.loc.gov/2021036410

Cherry Lake Publishing Group would like to acknowledge the work of the Partnership for 21st
Century Learning, a Network of Battelle for Kids. Please visit http://www.battelleforkids.org/
networks/p21 for more information.

Printed in the United States of America
Corporate Graphics